Praise for
Adjusting Your Sails

"This book is a beacon of hope, shining a light on the indomitable human spirit. It will reach deep within you, filling you with a sense of optimism and resilience. This is a story of survival and triumph over unimaginable trauma. If Lindsay found the courage and strength not only to survive, but to thrive, you can too. Wherever you are in your journey, this book will show you that there is hope, and that you can find help, whether through your faith or spirituality or resources that are available. Never give up!"
Terry Sidford, AAC. TEDx Speaker, Life Coach, Author
www.terrysidford.com

"WOW! What a beautiful way to depict life and the constant need for ever-changing sail adjustment. The reflection questions added an extra piece of self-reflection for me. I would definitely recommend this to all my friends in recovery."
Brian Neilson CPSS/ FPSS, Executive Director, Utah Association of Peer Support Specialists (UAPSS)

"Lindsay Jepperson's writing style is a pleasure to read, which conflicts beautifully with her painful story. Her words flow as smoothly as silk while she shares the story of her dysfunctional family, dangerous childhood, and young adulthood. Her reflection on life kept me mesmerized, unable to put it down. Highly recommend this story of resilience and self-improvement. It is a true story and it is inspiring."
Susan Thomas

"This story is very compelling. Not one dull moment. So many people will be able to relate to the author because she has had such a diversity of experiences, including being raped, divorced, going through mental, emotional, and physical abuse, being hospitalized, attempting suicide, dropping out of high school, using alcohol and drugs. I love how she found God and how He was able to help. So many psychiatrists think there is no cure for some mental health conditions, like borderline personality disorder, or other serious mental illnesses, but with God ALL THINGS are possible and that's the hope that this story conveys. I hope it will help a lot of people."
Kerri Ernstsen, Certified Peer Specialist and NAMI Utah HelpLine Expert for over 20 years

Adjusting Your Sails

Anchoring to God in the Storms of Life

Adjusting Your Sails

Anchoring to God in the Storms of Life

Lindsay Jepperson
with Wendy O'Leary

Surrogate Press®

Copyright ©2025 Lindsay Jepperson
All rights reserved.

No part of this book may be reproduced in any form whatsoever, whether by graphic, visual, electronic, film, tape recording, or any other means, without the express written permission from the author, except in the case of brief passages embodied in reviews and articles. This book is available at quantity discounts with bulk purchases for groups and organizations.
Note: Some names and identifying details have been changed to protect the privacy of individuals.

Published in the United States by
Surrogate Press®
an imprint of Faceted Press®
Surrogate Press, LLC
Park City, Utah
SurrogatePress.com

ISBN: 978-1-964245-16-4

Book cover and interior design by: Katie Mullaly, Surrogate Press®

Lindsay Contact Info
Email: runyoursuccess@yahoo.com
Instagram: @adjustingyoursailsbook

Disclaimer: The contents of this book are based upon the author's personal experiences. The insights, advice, and resources provided herein are not intended as a substitute for professional treatment.
If you are experiencing mental distress or suicidal thoughts,
please reach out and talk to someone immediately or call
the National Suicide Hotline 800.273.8255.

Dedication

To my husband Travis, your support, love and the belief
in me make everything possible.
Thank you for standing next to me in every chapter of life.

And to Haigen, Tate and Charley, you are my greatest
inspirations and my proudest stories.
May you always follow your dreams with courage and kindness.
This is for you- with all my love.
You are my favorite humans.

To myself, for finding the courage to heal out loud.
For choosing to turn pain into purpose
and vulnerability into strength.
This is a testament to my journey,
my growth and my unwavering commitment to
share my story God gave me - so others know
that they are not alone.
With love, grace and pride in how far I've come.

Continue to adjust your sails.

"He stilled the storm
to a whisper;
the waves of the sea
were hushed."

Psalms 107:29

Table of Contents

Forward 1

Part One: My Story

Introduction 7

Storms Early On - Chapter 1 9

Dark Clouds of Divorce - Chapter 2 11

Bleak Skies - Chapter 3 17

Calm Before the Storm - Chapter 4 22

Changing Winds - Chapter 5 26

Navigating Rough Waters - Chapter 6 29

Smoother Sailing Ahead - Chapter 7 32

Conclusion - Author's Note 35

Part Two: Workbook

Workbook Introduction & Tips 38

Storms Early On - Chapter 1 Questions for Reflection 41

Dark Clouds of Divorce - Chapter 2 Questions for Reflection 49

Bleak Skies - Chapter 3 Questions for Reflection 57

Calm Before the Storm - Chapter 4 Questions for Reflection 65

Changing Winds - Chapter 5 Questions for Reflection 73

Navigating Rough Waters - Chapter 6 Questions for Reflection 81

Smoother Sailing Ahead - Chapter 7 Questions for Reflection 89

Conclusion - Questions for Reflection 97

Resources 105

Acknowledgments 109

About the Author 110

About the Co-Author 111

Forward

*B*eing asked to write a forward to a book is quite an honor. An honor you never expect as someone's individual therapist. This is for many reasons. Mainly because your relationship with your client is confidential. In any situation outside of your office, you can neither confirm nor deny you even know your client—let alone disclose that you know them and have worked with them for seven years!

So, when Lindsay asked me to write this forward, I was quite honestly surprised and a little apprehensive. However, once I eased my clinical mind by having Lindsay sign, not one but two releases of information, legal documents allowing me to disclose and share confidential information from our therapeutic work together, I relaxed and realized what a unique opportunity this was to openly share praise about a client for their courage to pursue their hopes, fight for healthier relationships, work through and process trauma and mostly show up for themselves in the future.

I still remember when Lindsay called me to see if I was accepting clients. During our initial intake, I disclosed that we attended the same church and I wanted to make sure that this was something she would be comfortable with since we were likely to see each other. At the time, I lived in a small, rural town in Utah. It was not uncommon for me to run into my clients outside of my office. Actually, it was the norm. So, in my first appointments with clients, I address this scenario.

My "go-to" speech goes something like this: "There is a high likelihood that we will run into each other outside of this space. Our relationship is confidential in nature, so I will smile at you but I will not come up to you or wave. This is not because I do not want to see you or address you, it is to protect your confidentiality. I do not want you to have to explain who I am to someone if you are with others."

Adjusting Your Sails

I remember Lindsay saying she did not have any issue with us attending the same church. But she graciously said that if it made me feel uncomfortable, she would understand and would gladly take a referral to another therapist. Something struck me in that first conversation. Lindsay was highly aware, insightful, and incredibly conscious of my needs. Now, to be honest, this is a little uncomfortable for us therapists because we are supposed to be the ones to show up for our clients, not vice versa. That is our job.

Lindsay was different, though, and that was apparent from day one. The difference spoke to her awareness, sensitivity and thoughtfulness of others. By the end of the conversation, we both felt comfortable giving it a try and addressing any potential boundary or dual relationship issues that might arise.

My training is in clinical mental health counseling and I received my master's degree from Denver Seminary. From a young age, it was my desire to integrate my faith and my passion for helping people—the two were always linked. This is why Lindsay reached out to me. Lindsay's previous therapists did not have the faith integration specialty and this was something she deeply desired. I immediately felt this and knew Lindsay's story was part of an even bigger story. As she shared her past, she did so from a lens of where she had come from and where God had brought her to in the present. Her faith was her compass and her anchor.

Lindsay and I started working together in June of 2017, and very early on, I knew we were a remarkable fit. Sometimes you can just tell if a client feels comfortable with you. I could tell Lindsay felt comfortable right away. The rapport and trust were almost instantaneous.

Over time, she opened up about unimaginable experiences as a child and I learned about her resilience and tenacity as an adolescent. From getting emancipated as a teen and having never attended high school to becoming a highly esteemed teacher with a master's degree, having a beautiful family, and being well-known in our small community as a loving and caring person.

Faith-based counseling can be very powerful. Lindsay shared how her faith had transformed over the years and how she could look back and see how God had brought individuals into her life to guide her, protect her, and be the hands and feet of Christ in her life. She was also able to communicate how God may be able to use her story for His glory, which was incredibly inspiring.

Forward

As a person of faith, I don't believe God ordains unimaginable things to happen to us, but when they do, He can use them for His glory and to further His kingdom. Faith integration in counseling can bring purpose, hope, and meaning to circumstances outside of our control. Through faith integration in the counseling process, we recognize and identify that God is the Ultimate Healer. While we can do everything possible therapeutically within the walls of a therapist's office, we recognize that God is in control and He is always with us.

It is an awful reality, but unfortunately, it's true that with childhood trauma like Lindsay's, oftentimes there is a life of addiction, incarceration, homelessness, unemployment, and many other less desirable scenarios and outcomes. Lindsay overcame every challenge life threw at her and she did so with confidence, persistence, resilience, and resolution to be better and become better. From the first time she walked into my office, and throughout our work together, she was always an inspiration and I was always in awe of her strength of will and her perseverance. That never changed about her from day one.

As a trauma specialist, I often see the effects of trauma and specifically childhood trauma negatively affecting the adult lives of individuals. One of the most well-known trauma studies is the Adverse Childhood Experiences (ACE) Study, which was conducted by the Center for Disease Control and Kaiser Permanente. It explores the link between childhood trauma and overall health and functioning as an adult. In this study, they surveyed a number of individuals who had childhood trauma and looked at the long-term health effects across their lifespans. The study concluded that there was a strong link between the number of adverse childhood experiences to negative outcomes such as incarceration, poor physical health, mental health, increased rates of depression, poor academic performance, chronic health issues, and early death.

Lindsay took the ACE test in 2022 and scored a 9. There are 10 questions on the ACE test. Individuals who score a 4 or more are considered to have a "high risk" for toxic stress (ACES Aware). When I saw that, I was shocked. I would have never guessed Lindsay would have scored that high, even after working with her for five years by that point and knowing her story in depth. That just goes to show her commitment to herself, her mental health, her resilience, her courage, and her unwillingness to be a statistic. Lindsay is so many things AND she is NOT a statistic.

Lindsay is, however, a wonderful, intelligent, compassionate, and empathetic individual. She loves her children and family without end. She is an incredible friend to those around her. She is a once-in-a-lifetime teacher and educator. She is a mental health advocate. She is a warrior. She is a survivor. She is none of these things because she has to be, she is all of these things simply because she is Lindsay Jepperson.

I am so honored to have been part of her story. I am honored to have been a voice of support, encouragement, care, and advocacy, but most importantly, I am honored to have shared that holy space. The space where there are no words and only the Lord's presence and peace. The space where you feel seen, heard, and known. It is truly a privilege of a lifetime and one that I do not take lightly.

I hope the following pages inspire you. I hope they inspire you to see there is hope, even in the darkest of places. There is connection even in the thickest shame. There is healing, but you must have the willingness to stand up and walk toward it. May the following pages inspire you to do these things and know your worth. May you find connection, peace, and hope. May Lindsay's words be a light in the darkness.

And a quick note to Lindsay:

Lindsay,

You will never know how honored I am to have been part of your journey and part of your healing. The Lord works in incredible ways and I am so blessed to know you and to have witnessed all you have been through.

Your light is undeniable and your story is one that defeats all odds. May you continue to heal, grow, and experience all the Lord has for you. Thank you for allowing me to walk beside you and share that holy space. You inspire me and I know your story will inspire many more people than you can ever imagine. Thank you for being brave enough to speak the truth and know your true worth.

Lauren Hansen, LCMHC, LPC

Part One
My Story

"A lighthouse doesn't save the ships; it doesn't go out and rescue them, it's just this pillar that helps to guide people home."

Lea Michele

Introduction

Sometimes our past can wound us in ways that we can't ever imagine recovering from. Far too often, we give up on ourselves. I hope you will not do that because I know from personal experience that recovery and healing are possible, even against the greatest odds. As a person who has overcome multiple strikes against me, including being a "foster-care kid" and a high school dropout, who now has a loving family of her own, holds a master's degree, and has enjoyed a career as a special education teacher for more than seventeen years, I am a living testament that our pasts do not have to dictate our futures.

I believe the Grand Author of each of our individual stories is also writing an epic story that overarches, and yet includes, all our individual stories. Each of our stories is being incorporated and folded into a far grander story. Whether we realize it or not, there is a purpose for every page and every chapter in every one of our stories. These stories continue to unfold. None of our stories are without conflict or challenges. That is as it should be because without the struggle, the victory would be hollow or even non-existent.

The book you are reading is the story of my personal journey, through the ups and downs of life, and how I navigated through the storms and turbulence, making minor and major adjustments along the way to keep the "ship of my soul" afloat, intact, and heading in the right direction. From birth to where I am now, I have had to learn how to use the wind to steer my vessel through the storms of life and the battles that were destined to be part of my story.

Like you, sometimes I was successful in reading the winds and the weather, so I made good decisions that kept my vessel afloat and upright . At other times, the tide would turn, the winds would come up out of nowhere, and I would find myself being tossed and tumbled about in the turbulence. Sometimes I lost my way.

My story is about the things I learned along the way about righting the ship of my soul, about making adjustments to the sails of my soul, and trusting the ballast of my soul—the solid and enduring substance underneath all of the winds, waves, and weather that gave me the strength and conviction to endure.

I hope my story empowers you to reach out for help if you feel powerless. I hope it gives you the conviction that you are worth it if you feel worthless. I pray it gives you hope if you feel hopeless. The hope that you, too, can learn how to adjust your sails, right your vessel, and find and trust the ballast of your soul that knows you deserve a better life and the confidence that you can get there.

Telling your story takes vulnerability and courage because it leaves you open to being judged and criticized. I believe it's worth the risk.

The dream of sharing my story was born the day Jesus saved me. If my story only helps one person know beyond a shadow of a doubt that they are deeply loved despite the storms they are being tossed around in and if only one person can see that, then like me, they, too, can learn how to adjust their sails, fight the currents, and make it through the rain and the wind to a beautiful life they can hardly imagine right now. If only one person can come to know the depth of love that saves us, then telling my story will have been worth it.

I would like to emphasize that this is an account of how I experienced the events and relationships in my life and it is as accurate as my memory will allow. While I don't have any desire to hurt, embarrass, or offend anyone, I share the attitude of writer Anne Lamont, who said, "You own everything that happened to you. Tell your stories. If people wanted you to write warmly about them they should have behaved better."

Storms Early On
Chapter 1

I guess you could say that I started fighting the odds from day one. I was born on a cold day in December, frail and fragile, weighing only three pounds four ounces. My parents said I was rushed out of the delivery room as soon as I was born while the doctors frantically tried to save my life. I lived in the NICU unit of the hospital for the first twelve weeks of my life. I was finally able to go home when I reached a whopping five pounds. My grandmother told me I was so tiny they had to dress me in Cabbage Patch doll clothes.

My earliest memories are of a loving family—my parents, two sisters, and two brothers. We lived on a farm and while I don't have a lot of specific memories, I do fondly remember our horses, playing in the barn, and having picnics with both my grandmothers, who lived nearby and were extraordinarily loving and warm. I also spent a lot of time with my cousins and extended family.

At the tender age of eight, a tsunami crashed into my life, changing it and me forever. One night, my parents couldn't find a babysitter, so they asked a neighbor boy who was fifteen years old to babysit. After swimming and running through the sprinklers, he told us it was time to bathe. Of course, as an obedient eight-year-old, I listened to the babysitter and did what I was told.

One moment I was carefree and playing in the yard. The next moment my world went black. He had raped me. My childhood safety and innocence were ripped away from me forever. I remember crying and sitting by the window waiting for my parents to return.

I told my parents what happened. They seemed bewildered and didn't know what to do. They didn't want to call the police. Instead, they thought it would be best to call a religious steward in our area and consult with him on how to deal with this. He came over and talked with us. My dad was holding me. I was trembling. My mom was crying. He asked a few questions and then he promised to "handle it."

I never did find out how it was "handled" but there was never any type of confrontation with this young man, from either a religious or legal standpoint. I felt helpless and angry. I wanted someone to step in and hold him accountable for what he did to me and prevent him from harming others.

Dark Clouds of Divorce
Chapter 2

Despite this devastating experience that shattered my innocence and impacted my sense of self for years to come, my home life continued to be pretty simple and manageable. I still felt the love and support of my family and enjoyed spending time with my cousins and siblings. My grandmothers were my anchors, a harbor of safety and comfort. I loved baking homemade cinnamon rolls with Grandma Marge; I remember standing next to her in her kitchen all covered in flour and cinnamon. I loved going on picnics with Grandma Marge and taking trips up to the cabin where we would jam to Blue Jean Baby and be carefree.

Then, one day, the blue skies of childhood quickly faded as the abrupt dark clouds of divorce descended over our family. I came home from school in a particularly good mood, having enjoyed the day with my third-grade teacher, Mrs. Neilson. My mom and dad asked me to go sit down in the living room, along with my brothers and sisters. They said they had something to tell us while we were all together.

We were giddy with anticipation, fantasizing that we were about to learn about a wonderful vacation to Disneyland or that we were going to get a new puppy.

Instead, my parents carefully explained to us that they were getting a DIVORCE. I looked at my older sister, Megan, in bewilderment. I wasn't exactly sure what that word meant. I didn't know any other kids who had divorced parents. Yet, somehow I knew it wasn't a good thing that was about to happen to our family.

I tentatively asked, "What is a divorce?" Then I listened as my parents tried to explain something horrific as if it were a normal, rational, and logical thing to do. They were no longer going to be married to each other or live in the same house. They said optimistically that us kids would go back and forth and we would adjust and be fine. I couldn't comprehend this. I felt the anchor of my soul being ripped out of its mooring.

After they finished explaining how our lives would be forever changed, we all got up and set the dinner table, ate dinner, did homework, did our chores, and went about our bedtime routines as if nothing had happened. However, inside I was falling apart as I felt my world crumbling around me.

We kids had no choice but to adjust our sails to the changing winds of the back and forth between our parents' two homes. Dad stayed in our childhood home next to Grandma Helen's house. Mom moved across the railroad tracks to a new blue house. We spent one week with my dad and one week with my mom. Soon, both of my parents began dating new people and both remarried. I ended up with a bonus sister and brother with the remarriages .

Adjusting to the winds of remarriage was hard. I remember the day my dad remarried. By then, we were only seeing our dad on Wednesdays and every other weekend. He always made us feel loved and special during that time. I remember thinking that I had really lost him now that he was taking on a new wife and her two children. I just wanted all of this to stop.

During the reception, I ran and hid in a nearby field. The straw was covering me like angel's wings, protecting me from this new reality that I didn't want. I hoped my dad would discover that I was missing and cancel his honeymoon. Instead, after he found me, he still went on his honeymoon, but he lovingly reassured me that nothing would change before he left.

But it did, of course. Everything changed. My new stepmother tried her best to work with five extra kids around. My dad tried his best to keep everyone happy but his new wife was his primary focus now and he had two more children added to the mix as well. There was no longer time for my dad to spend with just us kids anymore. How I missed and longed for cherished time with just me and my dad, like when he would pick us up after school on Wednesday and we would pile in his truck and head to the family cabin—before the new wife came along. We always stopped at the gas station on the edge of town for a hot dog and a bag of chips to eat on the way. We would ride the four-wheeler, feed the cows, or fix a broken fence while we were there. No matter what we were doing, we had our dad's undivided attention. I always looked forward to going up to the cabin each week with my dad.

I also remember feeling dread and foreboding every time we left the cabin and my dad would drop us off at the blue house where we lived with our mom and her new husband.

The new husband was a giant of a man, and adjusting my sails began to mean the daily survival of his moods and temper. No matter how well-behaved we were, it didn't guarantee he wouldn't yell at us or call us names. The hostility toward us was palpable and unpredictable. One moment it seemed that everything was fine, but the next moment it felt like a torrent of hostility came unleashed and the tension of never knowing what to expect was unbearable.

I watched my mother's personality change from being carefree, happy, and enthusiastic to becoming a shadow of who she used to be. She used to light up the room and our lives. She was fun to be with, always thinking of creative things to do and make. I remember she made a majestic vision board detailing all the wonderful plans she had for her life and her children.

It was love at first sight when she met my stepfather. She fell fast and hard. She thought her dreams were coming true. She was almost giddy with excitement when they first began dating. I didn't mind him then. He seemed okay but I just had a feeling that something was wrong. Or maybe that it was too good to be true.

I hate that I was right about this. It broke my heart to watch my mother slowly fade away into this man's dominating presence as she tried to protect us and salvage her marriage at the same time. She lost her light and I lost my mother.

I started hating my stepfather when he began being hostile toward my dad and woueldn't allow him to come to the door to get us. He demanded that my dad pull up and honk for us. He was not allowed on our property. We would run to my dad as soon as we heard him honk and when he would drop us off, we would slowly drag ourselves back into my mother's home, feeling apprehension and dread.

When my stepfather started yelling at us kids, my mom tried to intervene, but instead, they just started arguing more. I couldn't stand it when he would yell at my younger siblings; it broke my heart watching their quivering lips and little bodies shake with fear. I remember a few times trying to intervene, but that only made him angrier. We never knew what would set him off, maybe slamming a door too hard or leaving something on the counter.

We walked on eggshells because of my stepfather's volatile moods. We lived off the bishop's storehouse, barely making it paycheck to paycheck. The only positive dynamic I remember during this time period was how closely knit the five of us siblings became . We watched out for one another and became protective of each other.

Often, we would retreat down to the basement to play together because it muffled the sounds of my mother and stepfather arguing and yelling. Their arguments became more and more frequent.

Every other weekend, we went to my dad's home and lived in luxury with gourmet meals that my stepmother prepared. My dad's home was immaculate—not one thing out of place. There was always some exotic aroma from an expensive candle and fresh flowers on the dining room table.

It was hard to go from one reality to the other. It was like living two different lives in two different worlds. And we children were supposed to be happy and well-adjusted because we still had both parents in the picture. On the surface, this seems logical and cultural norms seem to depict blended families living happily ever after. But in reality, in my experience and the experience of my siblings, this was not how it played out. Not even close.

I'm not saying that my parents should have stayed together or that every blended family isn't happy, but I believe life would have been much easier without all the halves, the steps, and the confusing brokenness that came to our family during this time.

After experiencing the trauma of being raped and the lack of protection from the adults in my life, I had turned inward. I was thankful for the love and protection of my siblings, but I still felt small and helpless much of the time, especially in the presence of my stepfather. He was a large man who was unpredictable and we were all afraid of him.

Living in two worlds, shuffling back and forth between two homes that couldn't be more different was disorienting enough, but the untenable stress of walking on eggshells around my stepfather with no hope of protection from his outbursts was too much. I didn't see a way forward. Life became bleak. I grew more and more depressed.

I started losing interest in the things I used to love. I used to love school and excel by getting good grades, but I couldn't focus and didn't care anymore. I was an avid soccer player but lost all interest in the sport. I also lost my passion and love for horses. I had been involved in Junior Rodeo and my dad had gotten me a beautiful buckskin. It was light brown, the color of a piece of toast. I remember how good I felt when I was with my dad riding horses—I was unstoppable. The world felt okay. I felt powerful and strong. But soon, I couldn't feel much of anything. The light that I watched fade from my mom started fading from me, as well.

My parents tried their best to get me involved in sports and other activities, hoping I would become interested and occupied. Nothing helped. By the age of twelve, I was on medication for *my* behaviors and *my* attitude problem. I was told that *I* needed to change, that *I* was causing problems. I was told that something was wrong with *me*. These messages only served to reinforce my belief that I was broken. I felt broken. I felt hopeless.

Looking back, I can see now that my behaviors and attitude were a desperate cry for help. Sadly, at that time, no one was listening.

My only refuge from the storm was my two grandmothers who would swoop in from time to time; they seemed to know when one of us kids needed a break. They invited us over for sleepovers, to go shopping, or just to enjoy a lunch date with them. They were my saving grace, coming to the rescue to give us a break from the craziness of our lives.

Grandma Marge, who we called Grandma Bug, smelled of flowers and sunshine. She would pick me up from school sometimes and I would slide into the front seat next to her. The radio was always playing. Her favorite group was the Oakridge Boys. I remember when the song "Blue Jean Baby" was released and my grey-haired grandma with hugs that melted you was sitting in the car singing it with me and my siblings, word for word.

Grandma Marge would bring me food or a new shirt she saw at the mall or a book she just knew I would love. She always had a craft or treat for us kids each time we visited. She had a saying, "I love you a bushel, and a peck, and a big hug around the neck." She gave hugs freely and made us feel loved.

Grandma Marge was big on journaling. During one of my hardest times, around the age of thirteen, I was helping her clean out a crawl space. We found a maroon journal from her high school days. It was such a treasure. We giggled as we read every page, sitting side by side at the table in her warm, welcoming kitchen.

Around that same time, my oldest sister started slipping away. I used to feel close and safe around her, but she started spending more and more time away from the house with her friends to avoid my stepfather. She was coping in her own way and there wasn't enough bandwidth for me. I felt abandoned. I was losing my father, my mother, my sister, and myself. It was unbearable.

One day, she announced that she was moving out and would be living with our dad and going to a different school. It felt like a black hole in my heart seeing her empty bed and knowing she was going to school on the other side of town instead of going to my school and coming home with me.

The abuse seemed to get worse after she left. My stepfather was furious. He began threatening us to not tell anyone what was going on in our home, saying it was private and nobody else's business.

After my sister moved out, I watched my mom sink lower and lower into a dark depression. My stepfather became more abusive. He crossed the line from verbally yelling at us to throwing things and threatening to hit us.

I remember the first time he hit me. My mom was not home. I said, "I am going to tell my mom." But he said, "She'll never believe you. She knows you are a little brat and a troublemaker." Then he locked us in the basement until she came home. When she walked in the door, we all had to "act" like everything was okay. He was pleasant and acted perfectly nice, as if nothing had happened.

Not only would he not allow my father to step on the front porch when he picked us kids up for visits, but he also began threatening him and cursing at him when he would come to pick us up. Visits with my dad became less and less frequent. My mom became more and more depressed. My stepfather's rageful behaviors grew worse and worse.

Bleak Skies
Chapter 3

I was thirteen years old the first time I made the decision that I wanted to die instead of continuing to live like this. I didn't know how else to stop the abuse, along with the unbearable emotional pain and the daily dread of what each day might bring.

I was sitting in math class when the school secretary came in and asked for Lindsay Miner. I walked out of the classroom and down the hallway with her. In the office was a slim lady with long, black hair waiting to speak to me. She had a folder in her hand. As I followed her into the principal's office, I thought I might be in trouble. She started asking me questions and writing down my answers in a little yellow notebook.

I had been questioned before, but this time my mom and dad were not there and it made me very nervous. It was just the principal, this lady, and me. I remember thinking, "Why now? Why me? What kind of trouble is this going to get me into when I get home?"

It was yet another investigation into allegations of abuse by my stepfather. It wasn't the first time. It had happened before, and as before, the investigation was found "unsupported" because my mother again covered up the abusive behaviors of my stepfather.

It was at this point that I remember thinking, "I can't do this anymore" and "there is no way out." That's when I knew what I had to do. I decided that ending my life was better than living like this. I went home from school and I took all my prescribed medication—three almost-full bottles of psychiatric meds, and I laid on my neatly made bed in my perfectly clean bedroom hugging my giant, stuffed gorilla and calmly waiting to die.

There were beads hanging in place of my bedroom door and I heard them rattling and saw my little sister come prancing in wearing a little blue romper with daisies on it and proudly displaying a picture she had drawn "just for me." She handed me a crayon drawing of sunshine and rainbows, and smiled at me, saying, "I love you" in a small, sweet, innocent voice.

At that moment, the winds shifted abruptly. I was overcome with emotion and suddenly I didn't want to die. I wanted to stay and protect my little sister. I hadn't felt any emotions in so long that I was surprised at how powerful the impact was.

I called a church leader and told her what I had done and told her I needed help. She instructed me to hang up and call 911 and told me she was on her way. It was all a blur after that as I was fading in and out of consciousness. The paramedics came and I remember laying on a stretcher being wheeled past my little sister and seeing her large eyes full of worry.

I was taken to a hospital that I had been to many times with my grandma. Only this time, my grandma wasn't wearing her little pink dress and showing me around. This time it was cold and stark and frightening. I was given a bottle of black liquid and was told to drink it. The nurse was kind and explained to me that it was charcoal and that it would make me vomit, which was necessary to get the poison out of my system.

I violently vomited black tar from my mouth for what felt like a very long time. My stomach and my throat were on fire and hurting beyond anything I can describe.

My father arrived at the hospital first. He was sympathetic and kind. Then my mother arrived a short while later. Soon after she arrived, they were arguing about whose fault it was that I had done this. Each began blaming the other.

The vomiting had subsided but the pain was still there, and most awful of all was the reality that I had almost taken my own life. I laid there holding my stomach and blinking back tears, feeling unseen and unloved. Finally, a very wise nurse stepped in and sternly told them both to stop. She said, "Look at this little girl lying here. Think about her from now on, not yourselves."

They paused for a moment, but unfortunately, for whatever reason, neither of my parents were able to take that nurse's advice to heart. They continued to argue and blame each other instead of connecting with me and finding out how I was feeling or what I needed.

After I was cleared medically, I was moved to the Pavilion, the psych unit for teens at Payson Hospital. Sadly, this would be the first of many attempts and the first of many times in this unit.

My hospitalization after this first suicide attempt was another time of adjusting my sails to meet the winds of reality. One day, I suddenly realized that if I wanted to get better, it would be up to me. I would need to start making my own decisions about what would be best for me and not wait for someone else to rescue me.

At times, I hoped maybe Jesus would. Before the divorce, my family had attended church, but after the divorce, it was hit or miss. My grandma was a woman of faith and would take us kids to church and prayed with us often. There was a picture of Jesus hanging in the bathroom of my mom's house, and even though it was just a generic picture, sometimes I would look into his eyes and know that somehow he was real and he wanted to help me.

I sensed—but didn't know how—that I would need to rely on God, not my own strength, to make it through. The reality also dawned on me that I couldn't live with my family, or at least not with my mom and stepdad if I wanted to heal.

Unfortunately, I didn't have much choice and had to go back to my mother's home to live. Nothing had changed. The insanity and abuse continued in my mother's home and my father continued to grow busier and more distant.

After I was home for about two months, trying my best to adjust to the storms of abuse and winds of despair that continued unabated, the anchor could not hold.

It all came crashing down one day. I ran away. I stayed in a trailer that belonged to a friend's family for a few days while everyone was searching for me. My friend, Nick, was one year younger yet much larger in stature than me. He knew a little about what I was going through at home and he genuinely cared about me. The day I ran away I was crying and poured out my heart to him, telling him how bad it really was at home. He held me while I cried big crocodile tears and we both agreed that I couldn't go back there.

He told me I could stay in his family's trailer on their feedlot while I figured something out. I was surrounded by cows and mud. It smelled horrible, but it was safe. There was a small couch and running water.

He borrowed some clothes from another friend and brought them to me along with some top ramen. We quietly ate the soup together. Then he kissed me on the forehead and said it would be okay. I really hoped he was right, but I was also afraid it wouldn't be okay. I was afraid to be found out because his mother didn't like me, saying that I was a bad influence and she didn't want me around him. He promised to check on me the next day and bring me more food. I was grateful for his compassion and care, but when he left, the darkness of the night and the heaviness of my situation crept over me. I felt scared and alone. I cried myself to sleep, unsure of what might happen next.

I laid low for a few days, but then I wanted to go back to school. Nick said he would come pick me up one morning. When I heard the rumble of his diesel truck outside, I left the safety of the trailer for the first time in days. I was only at school for a short time, when I was called to the office because the police were there. My dad had reported me as a missing runaway.

The police were kind. They knew I was one of the kids from "that family" who had several open child welfare cases. My dad had learned about me running away and had been helping the police search for me. The police asked if I felt safe going to my dad's while things got figured out. I said, "yes," and was overcome with relief that the police were not going to take me back to my mother's house where I was certain I would face unspeakable consequences and the wrath of my stepfather.

The judge gave my father and stepmother temporary custody and I was able to stay with them for a while. It was different being in a home that was fully furnished, had plenty of food in the fridge, and served a home-cooked meal every evening. Unfortunately, it didn't last long.

Within a couple of weeks, I was escorted from the house by police due to my reactive outbursts, which were perceived as aggressive behaviors that made my stepmother feel unsafe. I was taken to Vantage Point for an extended stay until there could be another court hearing to determine my fate or at least where I would live next.

While at Vantage Point, I experienced another adjustment to my sails. This one wasn't abrupt. It happened gradually as it dawned on me that I had no control over the situation in my mother's home. I couldn't stop the abuse. I couldn't count on anyone else to stop it either—not my mom, not my dad, not my relatives, not the police, not the school, not the people at the psych-hospital, not even the Child Welfare folks.

Though I had prayed to God for protection and believed He could save me, I didn't understand why no one was protecting me. Wasn't that what the adults in your life are supposed to do?

Somehow, deep inside, though, I knew I could still lean on God to give me the strength to do what I needed to do to get better, including making some tough decisions.

As I awaited my next hearing, the reality that I couldn't go back to my mother's home and be with my beloved siblings was a hard reality to face. I just knew, deep in my soul, that I could not live with my stepfather under the same roof ever again—or I would not make it.

At this point, I had run away multiple times, attempted suicide a couple more times, and stayed in residential facilities that were designated for "wayward" kids—those kids who would never make it in society. Life was dark back then. I believe that much of what I went through during this desperate time was blocked from my memory, which might be God's way of protecting me.

The weeks went by at Vantage Point and I settled into a groove, staying on the top level with lots of privileges. Vantage Point was a blessing in disguise and one of the first times I was given tools to navigate the rough waters I was in. By now, I was also a ward of the state. As such, I was assigned a guardian ad litem (legal guardian) and a caseworker.

I had some interesting roommates with various horror stories and tragic tales of their own to share. My family visited for group therapy sessions and sometimes they brought items from home. I missed my brothers and sisters so much, and I remember achingly longing for a "normal" family.

My time never came for a normal family. When my court date approached to make a custody determination, the judge did not think either of my parents' homes were suitable for me. They began looking for other placements instead. This meant that the court and social workers, along with my parents, were reaching out to all our relatives to see if someone was able to take a troubled teen for a couple of years until she turned eighteen.

Calm Before the Storm
Chapter 4

My Aunt Susan and Uncle John stepped in. I didn't have a relationship with them prior to this. All I knew about them was they lived in Salt Lake City and were avid skiers. My caseworker, a very nice lady named Michelle, helped me pack the few belongings I had at Vantage Point. She told me that I was going to move in the next day with an aunt and uncle that I didn't know. I was crushed. Although I knew it wouldn't be good for me, I had been hoping and longing to return to my family and be reunited with my siblings. But it was not to be. Instead, I had to adjust my sails to this new living situation.

Susan and John lived in a beautiful home in a ski resort town up Little Cottonwood Canyon. The huge picture window in their kitchen overlooked the entire valley. Susan was a vibrant blond whose smile and hugs melted away my worries. She was educated, advocated for me, and was on my side from day one.

Both Susan and John were wonderful to me the entire time I stayed with them. They got reading glasses for me and took me to the doctor to find out why I was having constant stomach aches, which we learned were from the ulcers I developed. They got me on the correct medication for the depression caused by my past trauma. I learned how to drive and got my driver's license, plus I worked on my high school diploma through an online program. Through John and Susan's network, I met some great friends who saw my potential and were a good influence on me. John and Susan paid for some of my continuing education credits.

Susan always told me she believed in me and I know she did. She always told me how amazing my eyes were and that she could see the good in me. She made me feel welcome in their home. I adored their two little boys. We would have dinner together every night, so I helped make dinner and clean up. Their home was marked by quiet and calm; there was never any yelling or screaming. Though they were not religious, they were loving and kind. They asked me what I wanted in life and they did their best to help me get it.

Despite this positive environment and the support they gave me, I still believed the lies about myself and that my future was doomed. That I would never amount to anything. That I was damaged beyond repair. I couldn't seem to escape from my past track record. I was also dealing with unhealed emotional grief and pain from past trauma and the recent loss of my family. I missed my siblings, grandmothers, and parents terribly.

I started working at Snowbird and started drinking alcohol with my friends. It was a huge hit. I could get drunk, numb out, and not have to deal with the darker realities of my life that made me want to die. My aunt and uncle tried to address my drinking problem multiple times, but it was no use. I was hooked.

One weekend, I was at a party and tried cocaine. My life began spiraling even further out of control after that. My aunt and uncle saw that I was on a slippery slope, and even though they did their best to help me, I wasn't willing to give up the friends, booze, and drugs that were helping me forget my painful past. They also had two young sons to think about. I felt that I had outstayed my welcome, so I packed up a few of my belongings and left. I moved into a place with some friends in Utah County.

The day before my sixteenth birthday, I felt the coldest and darkest storm clouds ever wrap around me. I felt immobilized, afraid, and alone. I called my dad and told him that I had moved out of my aunt and uncle's home. I asked for his help. Next, I called my caseworker, Michelle, and told her I would need help finding another place to live.

Later that day, my dad and Michelle both came and helped me pack my belongings. They took me to a temporary home run by the state while we were figuring out my next move. Court was coming up. I felt nervous. I knew the judge would be upset about some of my choices and I was worried about where my next placement might be.

My guardian ad litem and Michelle helped me obtain the resources I needed to get an apartment. I was sixteen at the time and knew I could count on state assistance for two more years.

I remember the first night in my new apartment all alone, feeling broken and watching my world spiral out of control as I tried my best to pull it all back together.

I worked one job after another so I would have money to fund my habit of smoking, drinking, and doing drugs. My first job was at a steakhouse twelve bus stops away, but after a short time , I couldn't keep up. I was spending so much time and energy just getting to and from work that I quit after two weeks.

My favorite job was at a developmental center, which served adults with severe disabilities. I loved this job. It's where I discovered that I had a passion for working with people who have special needs. I was working this job and attending beauty school for a while, but it all became too much and I quit beauty school.

I kept thinking that somehow things would turn around one day, and until then, I would just keep doing what I was doing to get by. After all, I was doing okay, all things considered. Maybe I was even doing a little better than I was when I was living with my stepfather.

Then, one night, someone offered me heroin. The world went black again. This time, it felt soothing. It was the only thing that offered me an absolute escape from the jagged pieces of myself that I was living with. It also made me popular. I had friends now and the boys loved having me around. It became the only thing that could mend my broken heart. Within a couple of months, I was down to eighty-two pounds and completely out of touch with reality. I had no intention to stop using heroin at this point.

Then the unthinkable happened. In one week, I lost five of my friends to "black heroin." We had all used the same batch of heroin together, yet they were gone and I was still here. It was devastatingly unreal. I vividly recall attending one of their funerals and the mother of the dead young man was standing at the pulpit and pleading with us young people to stop killing ourselves with drugs. She was crying and shaking. I felt the heartbreaking tragedy of her grief and it pierced me in a way that nothing had for months. I left the funeral and headed straight to an abandoned parking lot to get high.

That's when God intervened in my life.

I paused and looked up for a moment. I saw the most beautiful sunflower I had ever seen. It reached tall into the sky and the sun cast a warm glow on it. It was a perfect moment. The warmth from the sun also touched me and I sensed an overwhelming love embracing me. I was about to adjust my sails again to remain in this flow of love from God that wordlessly reassured me that I could do better and that I didn't need drugs to help me through.

Suddenly, I threw all my drugs and paraphernalia out the window, looked up a detox center, and drove straight to the LDS Hospital's Intake Unit.

I walked into the clinic and saw some of the most broken people I had ever seen in my life. I felt pity for them. Then I caught a glimpse of my reflection in a window as I passed by and suddenly realized that I was just as broken as they were.

I prayed harder than I ever had before that something inside me would change and that this string of bad luck, brokenness, and aloneness would somehow come to an end this time. I needed something to save me from my hopelessness and my despair.

Changing Winds
Chapter 5

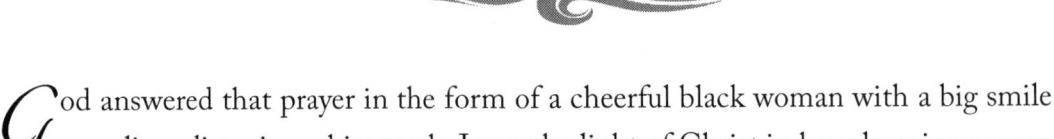

God answered that prayer in the form of a cheerful black woman with a big smile revealing glistening white teeth. I saw the light of Christ in her gleaming eyes as she kindly checked me in. Her name was Yolanda. She gently asked me some questions and then took me and my scant belongings to another room. She gave me some medications and told me they would help with my withdrawal symptoms, all the while reassuring me that I was going to be okay. Yolanda's hug was like being wrapped in a warm blanket of love and there was no denying this was straight from God.

My stay at LDS hospital was mostly a blur, as the demons and drugs left my body minute after painful minute. I had to drink a watermelon-flavored drink that caused me to vomit violently. My stomach felt like it was on the outside of my body. I was sweating profusely and my head was pounding.

Yolanda and the other kind ladies kept encouraging and reassuring me that in a couple of days I would feel like a new person. I swore to myself that if I survived this hell of withdrawing from drugs that I would never again touch the stuff.

God carried me through each painful day while I was detoxing. Finally, one sunny day, my detox time was up.

Yolanda came back to help me gather my belongings. She gave me some pamphlets and a Bible. She asked if she could pray for me and I said, "yes." I had never had someone pray over me and I knew I would need God's help to survive. My mind was blank and my stomach was empty. I was worried that anything I put into my body might cause my stomach to start having violent convulsions again. I felt dread and foreboding about what would happen next. I was relieved when she offered to pray for me. She held my hands and fervently prayed over me. She prayed for me to have strength to continue in my recovery, to overcome this evil addiction, and to be an overcomer in Christ. I thanked her and got one more of her motherly hugs before I grabbed my belongings and walked out of the detox unit.

Now what? I felt the warm sun on my face. I didn't know what to do next, but I knew from that moment on I would be okay if I kept focusing on and choosing the higher road. I knew good things would come my way one day if I held steady the sails of hope and kept remembering love's embrace that carried me from the abandoned parking lot into the detox center. I drove to a friend's house who did not use drugs. She was so proud of me for quitting and was willing to help me in any way she could. I stayed there for a couple of weeks until my next hearing.

The day of my hearing arrived. This was the hearing that forever changed my life. Judge Smith asked me to approach the bench, so I nervously walked toward him. He congratulated me on the time I had been clean and the classes I had taken, and he complimented my participation in the program. He said he had a plan for me. I dreaded hearing the words "foster home" but then he asked, "Would you like to be a part of a Youth in Custody program?"

I had no clue what that was. I was alarmed at the idea of not going home. Even though I knew it was unrealistic, deep inside I still longed to be with my family. Part of me was still hoping that somehow things might get better.

He described the Youth in Custody program saying I would have twelve months to complete the program before I would "age out" of the system, meaning I would turn eighteen years old and become a legal adult. Youth in Custody is a program that helps teens who have been emancipated from their parents. It pays for housing and food, plus it provides support for obtaining jobs and life skills like budgeting, shopping for groceries, and cooking. There are incentives for taking various classes and attending groups, like gift cards for groceries and/or cleaning supplies.

It sounded good to me. My case worker, Michelle, thought it would be a great fit for me. I accepted the offer and thanked the judge. We shook hands. He looked me in the eye and said, "You are one out of a hundred youth in this program. Make us proud!"

I packed my things and headed to the place that would be my home for the next twelve months. Michelle was very kind and helped me unpack, then she took me to the grocery store for food. After helping me get settled, she did what she always does at the end of our time together, she left. Left me alone in my new one-bedroom apartment.

But this time, I had new motivation, sobriety, and an opportunity to learn new skills and grow. I also wanted to make the judge proud and show my appreciation for this opportunity. The Youth in Custody program was an invaluable resource that I desperately needed to succeed. I learned how to plan meals, get ingredients at the grocery store, and cook for myself. I remember buying my first avocado and making guacamole for the first time in my little kitchen. I was so proud of myself! I was also working on high school packets with great enthusiasm. I had always loved school and learning. Unfortunately, I was unable to enjoy school while I was living in my mom's home with daily abuse and the stress it caused.

School was going well, but I was struggling with depression and anxiety and fighting for my continued recovery every day. I wasn't seeing my family at this point or hanging out with my old friends, so I felt lonely much of the time. I lacked the self-confidence of making new friends, which was hard to do without the social lubricant of drugs and alcohol. I was also dealing with daily heavy emotional pain from all the loss and trauma, and I didn't have the drugs and alcohol to help me numb out anymore. At times, I was tempted to 'use' again. But then I would remember the hell I went through detoxing and knew I never wanted to go through that again.

I prayed every day, every hour, that I could make it through and start feeling better about myself and my life. I wasn't in therapy or on any medications at this point. I was struggling but determined. This was what my life looked like for about eight months before I met my first husband.

Navigating Rough Waters
Chapter 6

The next big adjustment to my sails was adjusting to marriage. I met my first husband when I was cruising Main Street in Spanish Fork, Utah, one night. He was fun and he loved me. That's all I was looking for at the time—someone to fill that void I had deep inside for so long. We started dating and got married less than a year later so we could get the financial benefits of the Navy. I am not going to share much about my first marriage, but I like to tell people that I chose my first husband and God chose my second.

We moved to Whidbey Island, Washington soon after we got married; he was stationed there in the Navy. I was able to join a Christ-based recovery program on the base, which is where I accepted Jesus. For me, this experience was one of complete surrender. I knew that I couldn't manage my life, my addictions, and my painful emotions on my own, and I knew that God's will wasn't for me to suffer, but to shine. And the only way to shine would be to surrender daily to his will, not mine.

Every day I turned things over to Jesus and he consistently showed up for me. I had never experienced a consistency of love like this. Not only did God's love for me never waver, but I also didn't have to earn it or prove that I was "good enough" for God to love me. This was a new experience for me. It became easy to surrender to God.

I also met some of the most wonderful people in the world while we lived on Whidbey Island. I was blessed to find some true friends. It was also a blessing to be away from my family during this time. Though I still loved them very much, it was hard for me to be around them without becoming triggered and depressed. I still visited Utah when necessary, but it was good for me to get away and plant my two feet somewhere else.

One day while I was working, I met a woman named Rhonda. She was larger than life and outspoken, with a thick southern accent, not mincing any words. Her makeup and hair were impeccable. She was the definition of classy. One day, she asked me if I had ever considered going back to school to get a college degree. I hadn't finished high school at that point, so I told her that I was a high school dropout and couldn't get into college.

"We'll see about that," she piped up loudly, hands on hips. That night, she showed up with a college application, a credit card to pay for my first semester, and a notebook and pen for me so I could get started. To my surprise, I was accepted and started my first college class since dropping out of high school a few weeks prior.

Momma Rhonda took me under her wing and taught me some hard lessons. She had lived a tough life herself and taught me how important it was to keep seeing the good in life, no matter how bad it has been in the past. She loved Jesus and her prayers were mighty and bold. She saw the potential in me when I didn't see it in myself. She encouraged me and supported me. I eventually got a master's degree and became a special education teacher because of the faith she had in me even though I was a high school dropout. Her belief in me beating the odds shifted my own belief in myself. I will be forever grateful to her even though she is no longer with us.

Another blessing that came from living in Whidbey Island was the opportunity to serve at Service Alternatives where participants all had special needs. This launched me into my career as a special education teacher. I'll always remember the first special education classroom I walked into. There were little desks and a large cut-out calendar on the wall. I sensed a quiet excitement from the students as they eagerly welcomed me, a guest, into their space. Their smiles were like rays of sunshine penetrating my soul with their genuineness and their earnestness. My heart melted. One young man wore a helmet for drop seizures. He made his way over to me smiling. I introduced myself to him and the shrill squall he let out was one of pure joy. He motioned for me to come sit by him and I did. I knew this was where I belonged. This was what God intended for me to do.

I graduated college and then faced another storm. After my husband's two tours in Iraq and infidelity, I realized he was no longer the same man I had married. After trying to work things out during a brief separation, we divorced. I went to the legal office on base and started the process of a legal divorce. I felt shattered once again and my heart broke into a million little pieces. I didn't understand why I wasn't enough for him. I felt like a failure.

Navigating Rough Waters

I did have my relationship with Jesus, which sustained me through the rough waters of divorce, and after much prayerful consideration, I decided that moving back to Utah would be the best for me. I packed up my stuff into my dad's horse trailer and moved back. I felt broken and sad. However, this time, I also had confidence that God had something in store for me there. I adjusted my sails once more and landed in Heber City, Utah for a job at an elementary school.

Smoother Sailing Ahead
Chapter 7

My first couple years teaching special education in Heber City, Utah were challenging. Special education training includes one chapter on medically fragile children who have the potential to die in the classroom. I thought this was just standard training and didn't realize it would actually play out in my classroom. It definitely didn't prepare me for the deaths of two students and one of their siblings in my first two years of teaching. Nothing could have prepared me for that.

Darrin was an angel on earth. Watching him pass away from cancer was one of the hardest, and also most beautiful, experiences of my life. When his mother learned that he only had thirty days to live, she was the epitome of selfless love, sending him to school every day because he wanted to go, even though she wanted to hold onto him every one of those days. A couple months after Darrin passed away, his little brother who was in preschool died in a tragic accident.

Another of my students, a little girl who was struggling with disruptive behaviors for several months, was removed from my classroom. I was sad that we couldn't help her regulate and remain in the class. I got a call shortly after her removal saying that she had died of bone cancer. Though we didn't know it at the time, the bone cancer had likely been the cause of her outrageous behaviors.

I talked to my special education director and told her that I didn't think I could do this job because I was not equipped to deal with these kinds of tragedies. The winds of excitement that had propelled me into a career as a special education teacher had been taken out of my sails with the deaths of these three precious beings. I even imagined that it was a sign that moving back to Utah had been a bad idea, and I considered moving back to Whidbey Island. I mentioned this to a school secretary who I had adopted as my fairy godmother, and she begged me to give it one more year. She told me she had a very strong sense that I belonged here and that there was some reason I needed to stay.

I agreed to give it one more school year.

After burying three students in two school years at my elementary school,

Shortly after I was compelled to stay another year, I found myself sitting at a bar one evening next to a good-looking man named Travis Jepperson. I was grieving the loss of my students and admittedly, a little tipsy. I shared my story with him, and he shared his with me. He had been in a terrible accident and told me about the rigorous recovery journey he was on. We talked all evening about life, hopes, and dreams. At the end of the evening, we exchanged phone numbers, but I didn't think much of it. I certainly didn't expect to get a call from him.

I was surprised when he *did* call me a few days later. It was Mother's Day, a holiday I dread because of my estranged relationship with my own mother. He asked me out. I said yes.

When he showed up at my door, I realized that I had been clueless at the bar when he had been telling me about his accident and the recovery he was going through. I learned more about it and him on our first date. We went to dinner and I was fascinated by his story, what he went through, and his determination to walk again without braces or canes. I was in the middle of a master's program and he was in the middle of an intensive physical therapy training program.

We left our first date, which was at a small local diner, feeling a connection. We had bonded over our common habits, hurts, and hang-ups, but we believed we were both too busy to pursue a dating relationship at that time.

Somehow, we ended up married eight months later. Travis, despite his broken body, took my broken pieces, one by one, and showed me love and acceptance every single day. He showed me what a marriage is supposed to look like. He has been beyond patient with me and continues to encourage me to be the best version of myself. We have been married for fourteen years and have had our share of challenges. What I love about us is that we always try to climb the hills and scale the mountains together.

We have been blessed with three of the best gifts I could ever have hoped to receive, our precious children, Haigen (14), Tate (11), and Charley (9). Adjusting my sails to motherhood was another huge adjustment, however, to recount that would take an entire other book!

Conclusion

I wish I could end this story by tying it up in a neat little bow, describing how I've come full circle and have great relationships now with my whole family and that we were able to repair all the damage from when I was growing up. Unfortunately, that's not how things worked out. Some of these relationships are mended, some are partially mended, and others are worse than ever and will never be mended in this lifetime. That's the reality that I adjust my sails to every day.

The thing that has anchored me through all the ups and downs, the highs and lows, the traumas and triumphs, the stormy weather and rough waters, the times alone and adrift, has been my dependence on my loving Heavenly Father whom I know I can count on. He will never let me down, never hurt me, never disappoint me. Unlike earthly fathers, who may or may not be there for us in our times of need, our Heavenly Father is always there for us.

I continue to adjust my sails every day as new problems crop up and new challenges arise. I have struggled with addictions and eating disorders my whole life. I know that I can make it through only if I depend on my Heavenly Father. I do my best to adjust and then give it to Him.

Learning to trust and rely on our Savior, Jesus Christ, requires a willing heart and mind. During your storms and dark times, I hope you will seek the only true lighthouse, Jesus Christ, to deliver you. You will also need some practical skills, tools, and resources, which you will find in the next chapter .

Author's Note

Part Two of this book is a companion workbook. It contains questions for reflection to help readers reflect on their own journey and how they might be able to adjust their sails to the storms of life. There are blank pages for you to write or journal in. You can use this workbook personally as a journaling tool or you can use it to facilitate small group discussions.

Whatever you do, though, don't give up. Keep adjusting your sails. Reach out for help. Tap into available resources. And remember Jesus loves you and wants to help you navigate through your own stormy trials and bad weather.

Hang in there! You've got this!

Jesus, be the center,
Be our hope,
Be our song,
Jesus, be the fire in our hearts,
Be the wind in our sails,
Be the reason we live, Jesus.

Part Two
Workbook

Workbook Introduction & Tips

Welcome to the workbook section. I have shared my story with you because I would like to help others who are struggling right now. I want you to know that there is always hope that things can get better.

I know your journey is different than mine and not everything in my story will be relatable to your story. But no matter what, I know that there is a way through for you. I also know that drugs, alcohol, and suicide are not the answer to your suffering.

I am hoping and praying that this workbook will give you a place to start because I know that without doing the inner work of reflecting, reaching out for support, and earnest efforts to make changes, nothing will change. Not even with God's spirit upon us, guiding us, strengthening us, and comforting us. We must also do the work of healing.

If you aren't sure about God's love for you or willingness to help you, I suggest that you still do the work, reach out for help, and pray for God's spirit to be with you. Sometimes, when we are in the depths of despair, and sometimes due to the very trauma that put us there, we cannot receive love, not even God's. But be assured, God does love you.

Remember, too, that God works through other people - people who genuinely care about your wellbeing and want to see you pull through and come out the other side victorious. I know how hard it can be to ask for help and even harder to trust, after you've been let down, hurt, and betrayed by those who claimed to love you. Yet, it's essential to learn how to find safe and supportive people who care about you for genuine healing to take place. You can't do it alone.

Workbook Introduction & Tips

If you don't want to go talk to a therapist, consider meeting with or talking to a peer support. This is someone who has struggled with their own mental health and/or addiction issues and they have achieved a measure of healing and now want to support others who are a few steps behind them on their journey. Or talk to a trusted loved one, friend, family member, or faith leader. There are also talk and text lines you can access if you don't feel safe or comfortable confiding in someone you know.

Just don't try to go it alone.

Your friend,

Lindsay Jepperson

P.S. Even when it feels messy, painful, and confusing, keep going. Romans 8:28 says, "All things work together for the good of those who LOVE God, to those who are called according to His purpose."

Storms Early On
Chapter 1 Questions for Reflection

Many people think that young children do not understand rape or sexual abuse. Because of this, they ignore the devastating impact and lasting damage this type of abuse has on an innocent child. These norms may also endorse allowing religious leaders to resolve issues of abuse privately within the family or religious community. This causes the abused child to go unsupported in dealing with the emotional aftermath—not knowing how to overcome the stress and fear of being violated again, cope with the shame of what happened to them, or learn how to process what this means. This often leaves the child feeling damaged for life and alone, they're unable to talk about it, and they perhaps even blame themselves. All of this makes it impossible to heal and recover.

My personal experience, as well as others with similar experiences, proves that this approach to the sexual abuse of children is not sufficient to correct the perpetrator or help the child heal and recovery. The belief that small children do not understand what happened to them is false and extremely damaging to everyone involved.

1. Do you have one or more experiences from your early childhood that caused you to believe you were damaged for life? Does it still affect you today? If so, how? Have you addressed the trauma with a trusted mentor or professional?

2. Have you ever been victimized and then the person who harmed you wasn't held accountable? If so, how did that experience affect your ability to heal and recover?

Adjusting Your Sails

Storms Early On Reflections

Adjusting Your Sails

Storms Early On Reflections

Adjusting Your Sails

Storms Early On Reflections

Adjusting Your Sails

Dark Clouds of Divorce
Chapter 2 Questions for Reflection

Societal norms may say that it is healthy and positive for children of divorced parents to move back and forth and have access to two parental homes. I wonder if the experts who decide on these "norms" have ever had to experience what this is really like—being shuffled back and forth between two homes that couldn't be more different in rules, expectations, and environments.

Although experts claim that children are not harmed by divorce or adversely impacted by living in single-parent homes or stepfamilies, that was not my experience. Nor has it been the experience of many people I've talked to.

As children, disruption in the family caused by divorce is often, if not ALWAYS, painful, confusing, and stressful. Children often feel unloved and unwanted by one or both of their parents. The drastic changes that come in the aftermath of a divorce are overwhelming to most children and they are adversely affected.

Just because divorce is normalized in our society, does not make the impact of it any less painful for the children involved.

1. Have you experienced the divorce of your parents or loved ones? If so, how did it affect you and your life when it happened? How does it affect you now?

2. Have you experienced being a part of a step-family and/or living in two different homes due to divorce? If so, what did you learn about yourself and life from this experience?

Adjusting Your Sails

Dark Clouds of Divorce Reflections

Adjusting Your Sails

Dark Clouds of Divorce Reflections

Adjusting Your Sails

Dark Clouds of Divorce Reflections

Adjusting Your Sails

Bleak Skies
Chapter 3 Questions for Reflection

Societal norms would suggest that I was doomed to repeat the same pattern of behavior for the rest of my life. That was the message I received so many times, in so many ways, by so many people over the years—and I came to believe it. I came to believe that I was one of those "troubled kids" and that was my fate. Thankfully, in time, the faith and healing resources offered to me became a healing balm that allowed me to beat the odds and shake the identity of "troubled youth."

1. Are there any negative beliefs about yourself or any labels you've been given that have been hard to shake or let go of? If so, how do you think you could begin to think differently about yourself and what's possible?

2. If you do have a label that you've identified with, please describe yourself without referring to that label. Who are you, without that label?

3. How would you like to see yourself and how would you like others to see you? What can you do today to move in that direction?

Adjusting Your Sails

Bleak Skies Reflections

Adjusting Your Sails

Bleak Skies Reflections

Adjusting Your Sails

Bleak Skies Reflections

Calm Before the Storm
Chapter 4 Questions for Reflection

There is clear statistical data showing that outcomes for kids in the foster-care system do NOT have positive life outcomes. Most end up addicted, homeless, incarcerated and/or taking their own lives. Even when they are extended love from well-intentioned foster families, adoptive families, and/or next of kin relatives, these kids have a difficult time receiving and trusting the love and care extended to them. Sadly, many 'act out' behaviorally, validating their beliefs about their unlovability and/or their distrust of adults and authority, sabotaging the opportunities they are given.

1. Have you experienced not being able to receive or accept loving support or help in your life? If so, do you understand why you weren't able to let the loving help in?

2. Have you ever experienced instances of sabotaging your own success? Or times when you participated in destructive behaviors that you knew were harmful to yourself? If so, were you able to make sense of what was driving your sabotaging and/or self-destructive behaviors?

Adjusting Your Sails

Calm Before the Storm Reflections

Adjusting Your Sails

Calm Before the Storm Reflections

Adjusting Your Sails

Calm Before the Storm Reflections

Adjusting Your Sails

Changing Winds
Chapter 5 Questions for Reflection

Many of us find it hard to face ourselves and harder still to accept help. Not facing ourselves means we are not able to find the needed motivation and courage to change, and not accepting help means we will probably not be able to make any changes even if we really want to. Facing reality and accepting help are two keys to making beneficial changes in our lives.

1. Do you recall a time in your life that you decided to make a change and then followed through? What motivated your change?

2. Have you ever had the experience of accepting help from other people to make an important change in your life? If you haven't accepted help, do you know why?

Adjusting Your Sails

Changing Winds Reflections

Adjusting Your Sails

Changing Winds Reflections

Adjusting Your Sails

Changing Winds Reflections

Adjusting Your Sails

Navigating Rough Waters
Chapter 6 Questions for Reflection

During a season of learning and growing, we often meet many individuals who each help us in a different way. Some are there for a season – teaching us a lesson and helping us grow. Others become lifelong cherished friends.

We don't always know the reasons or seasons for some people in our lives but we do know that remaining open to learning from each one, we can grow and accept opportunities that we would otherwise miss out on.

1. Who has come into your life, temporarily or long-term, and had a significant impact on you that helped you learn and grow?

2. What have you learned about yourself in the different relationships you've been in?

Adjusting Your Sails

Navigating Rough Waters Reflections

Adjusting Your Sails

Navigating Rough Waters Reflections

Adjusting Your Sails

Navigating Rough Waters Reflections

Adjusting Your Sails

Smoother Sailing Ahead
Chapter 7 Questions for Reflection

I've been blessed, it's true. However, the odds were against me. I came from an extremely dysfunctional background, experiencing emotional, physical, and sexual abuse before entering the foster care system and the dark world of drug addiction. I know what it's like to be labeled and judged as "no good" and to want to die because of the hopelessness of my situation.

I believe I survived because I didn't give up. However, I believe I truly began thriving when I let other people in and began to accept help. I believe God works through other people, and when I realized how much God loved me, I was able to look back and see all the ways he had always been guiding me to the right places, people, and resources. He was always with me, but I didn't always know it.

1. Have there been times in your life when you believed that no one cared about you, not even God?

2. When you look back on your life, can you see any instances where God was working through other people to try to help you? Did you accept or reject that help?

Adjusting Your Sails

Smoother Sailing Ahead Reflections

Adjusting Your Sails

Smoother Sailing Ahead Reflections

Adjusting Your Sails

Smoother Sailing Ahead Reflections

Adjusting Your Sails

Conclusion
Questions for Reflection

How can you adjust your sails today? What is one resource that might help you do that?

1. How can you adjust your sails today?
2. What is one resource in the Resource Section that might help you do that?

Adjusting Your Sails

Conclusion Reflections

Adjusting Your Sails

Conclusion Reflections

Adjusting Your Sails

Conclusion Reflections

Adjusting Your Sails

Resources

Crisis Resources

988 - If you or someone you are with is experiencing a mental health crisis, please call, chat, or text 988. This is 24/7 confidential support for persons in distress and/or at risk of hurting themselves or others.

You can press 1 for Veterans
2 for Spanish
3 for LGBTQ+

You may request a **Mobile Crisis Outreach Team (MCOT)** at no cost to the individual. The team usually consists of a therapist and a peer support specialist who will try to stabilize the person in their own home and/or the least restrictive setting. NOTE: MCOT is not available in all areas.

Check your area for **Mental Health Crisis Receiving Centers** and/or you may walk into any **Hospital Emergency Department** 24/7. It's a good idea to have this information on hand before a mental health crisis situation develops.

Note: If someone has ingested something poisonous or has a weapon, please call 911.

Warm Lines

NAMI National HelpLine can direct you to local resources and warm lines. 800.950.6264 or text "helpline" to 62640
https://nami.org

NAMI National Warmline Directory
https://www.nami.org/NAMI/media/NAMI-Media/Helpline/NAMI-National-HelpLine-WarmLine-Directory.pdf

Mental Health America
Find your local chapter and/or national resources.
https://mhanational.org/crisisresources

Warmline.org is a directory to help you find the right help, staffed by peer support specialists.
https://www.warmline.org/#directory

Alternatives to Suicide Support Group
A peer-led support group that allows participants to discuss their suicidal feelings, thoughts, and experiences without fear of being judged.
https://www.mhawisconsin.org/alt2su
Read more about Alternatives to Suicide Approach here:
https://www.communitypsychology.com/new-approach-to-suicide/

Resources

Addiction Recovery Resources

SAMHSA (Substance Abuse and Mental Health Services Administration)
National Helpline 24/7 365 Treatment Referrals. Find help by calling #800.662.HELP.
https://www.samhsa.gov/find-help/national-helpline

Partnership to End Addiction
Information about different types of recovery support groups for addiction, including 12-Step, SMART (self-management and recovery training) Recovery, MM (Moderation Management), and additional addiction support group models.
https://drugfree.org/article/recovery-support-groups-for-addiction-one-size-does-not-fit-all/

National Institute on Drug Abuse
Everything you need to know about addiction recovery programs and processes.
https://nida.nih.gov/research-topics/recovery

Addiction: Choosing the Right Place for Treatment (from WebMD)
https://www.webmd.com/mental-health/addiction/features/addiction-choosing-rehab

Celebrate Recovery
A safe place to find Christ-based support for your hurts, hang-ups and habits (including addictions).
https://celebraterecovery.com/

Peer Support

Peer support workers/specialists are people who have successfully recovered from a mental health condition and/or a substance use disorder and are trained to help others who are experiencing similar challenges. Most States have a Certification program for peers and family peer support through their Department of Health and Human Services. Check with your State's DHHS and see if Peer Support is available in your area.

National Association of Peer Support Workers - Directory
https://www.peersupportworks.org/community/connections/national-registry/

SAMHSA (Substance Abuse and Mental Health Services Administration) About Peer Support
https://www.samhsa.gov/sites/default/files/programs_campaigns/brss_tacs/peer-support-2017.pdf

Recovery International
The mission of Recovery International is to use the cognitive-behavioral, peer-to-peer, self-help training system developed by Abraham Low, MD, to help individuals gain skills to lead more peaceful and productive lives.
https://www.recoveryinternational.org/

Wildflower Alliance
A grassroots Peer Support, Advocacy, and Training Organization
https://wildfloweralliance.org/

Christian Peer Network
Trained Peer and Family Peer Support volunteers who provide practical support and spiritual encouragement to those struggling with their own or a loved one's mental health challenges. This mental health peer ministry is provided through participating churches. For more information, please contact the network.
Phone: 385.452.3236
Email: *christianpeernetwork@gmail.com*

Acknowledgments

Along with my amazing family, I want to give a shout out to one of my students, Gauge Crumpton, who has become my official lead cheerleader, consistently and constantly encouraging me to finish this book and tell my story.

From the bottom of my heart I want to thank my two therapists, Lauren and Bobbie, who each helped me on my journey to do the inner work I needed to do – not only to heal, but to be able to open up and share even the hardest parts of my story so that I can 'give back' and hopefully it can help others. I wouldn't be where I am today and I would not have been able to openly share my story if it weren't for their wisdom and their valuable help on my healing journey.

I also want to thank Wendy O'Leary who came along at a critical juncture when I was hopelessly stuck in the writing process. She helped me pull the memories, the words, and the parts of my story together into a cohesive whole – the book you are now reading.

Momma Rhonda is no longer here to thank, but I know she looks down from heaven and is proud of what I have done with the opportunity she gave me. I got my master's degree and have been a special education teacher for over seventeen years thanks to her support and encouragement. I was a high school dropout, a product of the foster care system, and a recovering drug addict, yet she didn't see all of that. Instead, she saw me. And she believed in me, even when I didn't. She saw my potential when I couldn't. I will be forever grateful for this woman's impact on my life.

About the Author

Lindsay Jepperson is passionate about telling your story and dedicated to healing and growth. Through sharing her personal story she creates space for others to feel seen, heard and empowered through the power of Christ. A devoted wife to a hunk and mother to three, she finds inspiration in everyday moments with her family- Haigen, Tate and Charley are her biggest blessings. With a heart for connection and a belief in the power of vulnerability Lindsay reminds us all that healing is possible and our stories matter.

About the Co-Author

Wendy O'Leary has been working in the mental health field since 2007 working directly with families, as well as training and supervising family support staff. She became interested in this work because her own young son was struggling with mental health challenges and a serious brain injury.

In her work, she has trained dozens of people to effectively share their stories of healing in a way that fosters connection and inspires hope.

Wendy has written professionally for regional and local magazines and newspapers. She enjoys working with authors to help them share their healing journey. She is available for freelance writing work and may be contacted at *wendymoleary@outlook.com*.

Made in the USA
Columbia, SC
02 April 2025